The Golden Wing

Where Souls Remember

Sanila Jacob

BookLeaf
Publishing

India | USA | UK

Made with ❤ on the BookLeaf Publishing Platform
www.bookleafpub.in
www.bookleafpub.com

Dedication

For the one whose light found me beyond lifetimes,
whose touch still stirs the oceans in my heart.
You came like a whisper,
stayed like a prayer,
and became the pulse between my every breath.
Even after the wings closed,
you kept me golden.

Preface

This book is born from love that refused to end.
It began with two souls who met on earth for a little
while, but continued their story beyond time, beyond
flesh.

Each poem in these pages carries a piece of that light —
the warmth of his smile, the ache of his absence, and the
quiet strength that love left behind in me.

"The Golden Wing" is not about loss, but about how love
transforms us, how it teaches us to see beauty even in
pain, and how the soul, once touched by another, can
never be the same again.

If you have ever loved deeply,
if you have ever longed beyond reason,
may you find yourself somewhere between these lines —
and feel that the wings of love never truly fall.

Acknowledgements

To the One above,
for giving me strength when I had none,
and for letting me find meaning in what was left behind.

To my family and friends,
who stood quietly beside me while I learned to breathe
again.

To every soul who has ever lost someone
and still found the courage to love the world —
this book is also for you.

And to the one who became my light,
my muse, my golden wing —
your love still guides my every word,
your memory still keeps me alive in gentleness.
You are thanked in every heartbeat of this book.

1. Echoes of the Unfinished

Life's canvas remains
unfinished, threads of
thought dangling like
mid-air melodies.
Unwritten books,
unpainted masterpieces,
and unsung poems linger,
echoing the whispers of what could
have been.
Conversations suspended, tales untold,
and the silence that follows haunts,
astonishes, and
perplexes.
In the spaces between,
memories linger,
refusing to fade

2. In the Breath of Nature

"I've searched for you in every whisper of the wind,
In forest depths, where ancient secrets spin,
In rain-kissed petals, and the breeze's gentle touch,
In streams that flow like memories, and nature's tender
clutch.

I've looked into the eyes of strangers, friends, and trees,
But your presence, like a mirage, remains elusive to me.
Still, I'll wander, searching, through life's ebb and flow,
For the fleeting glimpse of you, that only whispers low."

3. To Love a Dying Flower

"A wilting flower, petals worn,
Fading fast, yet love is born.
In fragile beauty, we behold,
A life that's fleeting, love that's told.

Can we cherish every fragile breath?
Love the flower in final death?
Does love's depth measure in fleeting time?
Or does it bloom in love's last rhyme?

Perhaps in fading light, we see,
A beauty that transcends mortality.
The flower's last bloom, love's pure fire,
A love that's fierce, and heart's desire."

4. Lost and Found in Rain

"Time unfurls, yet sorrow deepens,
Like gathering storm clouds, my heart thickens.
The love I hold for you, an unrelenting downpour,
Drenching me completely, every fiber, every hour.

In this tempest of emotions, I find solace and peace,
The chill of longing, the wetness of love's release.
For in this deluge, I'm lost, yet found,
Submerged in the depths of my love for you, unbound."

5. Threads Beyond Time

I don't think we just met —
I think we collided,
two stars that remembered
the glow of another sky.

Your soul felt like déjà vu,
a whisper from lives I can't recall,
yet my heart understood
its language by instinct.

Every glance was an echo,
every touch a memory
neither of us could name,
yet both of us could feel.

Perhaps we had debts of love left unpaid,
or promises carved into eternity
that no death could erase.

They call it karma —

but this was something purer,
something that burned not to teach pain,
but to awaken what sleeps in the soul:
the knowing
that love is infinite.

6. The Journey of Becoming

"I have walked this Earth in many forms.

I have been the woman with empty arms.
I have been the child who died too young.
I have been the mother who waited for letters that never
came.

I have burned with grief.
I have danced with joy.
I have kissed someone I'd never see again.
And I have sung to the stars when no one else was
listening.

In this life... I asked for love that would **not bind me**,
but awaken me.
And I found it — in *him*.

He was not mine to keep.
He was mine to love.

Now he has gone home.
And I am still here — finishing the prayer we began together.

I do not need to be remembered.
I only need to *remember who I truly am.*

I am a soul of light.
I am not lost.
I am nearly done.

And when it's time... I will return home,
not with tears,
but with peace.

I am love.
I am light.
I am free."

7. The Real Dream

I believe every soul should fall in love—
Not the kind dressed in promises and petals,
But the kind that burns quietly in the chest,
That strips you bare,
That makes you weep in silence and sing to the wind.

A love so pure, it unhooks you from the world—
From the chase, the noise, the glittering lies.
A love that teaches you:
There is nothing to own,
Only moments to hold.

When you love like this,
Greed falls away.
You stop wanting gold,
And start longing for moss beneath your feet,
The hum of bees,
The sunlight resting on your eyelids like a kiss.

You stop dreaming of mansions and cars,

And start dreaming of someone's breath beside you in
the dark,
Of hands intertwined beneath stars,
Of a soul that recognizes yours—even when nothing is
said.

Only in this kind of love do you see:
The real dream was never in the cities.
It was always in the wild silence—
The stormy hills, the trembling trees,
The river that carries grief without question.

I have known this love.
I have lost it, and yet it lives in me still.
Now, even alone,
I am never truly alone.

Because the breeze remembers his name.
And the birds, they carry his smile.
And the sky?
The sky holds every unsaid word.

8. I Left Her Whole

I sat across from her,
the woman who held the boy I loved
before I even knew his name.
She smiled, trembled,
touched my lap as if my skin
might carry some echo of him.

And I—I wanted to pour oceans,
to say *He was mine too,*
to place every secret moment in her hands,
but her palms are already bleeding
from the weight of goodbye.

So I swallowed my truth like glass.
I let her think I was only quiet,
not a cathedral of broken vows.
Because love, real love,
sometimes chooses silence
over the sound that could ruin
what little light remains.

And when she said,
"You don't talk like before,"
I only smiled,
while a thousand words clawed
at the back of my teeth.

I left her whole—
and myself, in shards.

9. The Butterfly and the Flower

A butterfly, his wing almost gone,
so fragile in the heavy, chilling wind,
sat quietly, as if the storm was music.

The flower leaned close and asked,
"Why do you rest here, love, in this cold?"

He smiled with tired grace and whispered,
"Let me feel it —
the wind, the chill, the wild breath of the world.
One last time."

And the flower, my heart,
watched him shimmer in that moment,
knowing it was the last time
he drank beauty so deeply.

If only the breeze carried him joy,

I hope he left this earth
with happiness brushing his wings.

10. The Sun I Loved

Some people are like flowers—
they rise with the morning,
unfolding their light to the sun,
and all day they dazzle,
enchanting the butterflies
who dream only of their touch.

But evening comes,
and with the hush of dusk they fade,
stealing our hearts as they go.
Yet in their passing
they leave a mark eternal,
an imprint etched in golden ink
upon the soul.

11. The Weather of My Soul

My mind drifts like the weather —
once mine to calm, now its own wild sea.
It changes like October rain,
soft one moment,
then breaking open suddenly.

At dawn, light spills through me,
warm, forgiving, gold.
But by noon, the sky grows heavy,
and clouds begin to fold.

No one can read this shifting sky.
Some call it grief,
some call it weakness,
some call it madness whispered low.

But they do not know —
this storm has a name.
It is Love.
The rain that won't end,

the thunder that hums a memory,
the wind that still carries a voice.

And though I cannot command the weather anymore,
I let it move through me —
for in every storm's ache,
love still breathes.

12. Even If I Lose a Wing

Once a butterfly asked a flower,
"Will you still love me,
If one day my wings are torn,
And I can no longer dance in your sky?"

The flower swayed in the quiet breeze,
And whispered,
"You are the same soul
Who brought me spring,
Who brushed me with magic when the world was still.
Wing or no wing,
You will always be the song in my petals."

And nearby, a dragonfly rested,
Its broken tail still shining,
As if to say —
Love remembers us whole,
Even when we are not.

13. The Flowers I Brought You

Today, I brought you flowers, love—
not because the earth forgot you,
but because my hands needed to remember.

Each petal, a breath I held for you,
soft as the words I never finished.
The roses leaned toward your silence,
as if they knew your name in their veins.

I set them down, and for a moment,
it felt like placing my heart
on the altar of the sky.

Even the wind slowed,
as if to read our story in color—
pink for the tenderness we never spent,
white for the forever we still hold,
green for the life we promised,
rooted beyond endings.

I walked away empty-handed,
but heavier with love,
because flowers die—
and we do not.

14. I Don't Fear Death Anymore

I don't fear death anymore,
I'll embrace it when it comes with grace.
Because I'm longing for home—
Heaven.
Where my heart is.

Where love never ends,
Where pain has no name,
Where I'll see him again,
And nothing will be the same.

I've walked through fire with a smile,
Held tears like flowers in my chest,
But now,
I just want rest.

Not in sorrow,
But in surrender.
Not in darkness,

But in light so tender.

He waits there.
And I?
I am only walking him home—
Step by step,
Through each breath,
Until death
Becomes reunion.

15. When I Come Home

Since the day you left, I've been searching —
through wind that hums your name,
through the hush between the waves,
through the glow that lingers after sunset's flame.

The wind knows where you're hiding,
the sun remembers the path you chose.
The moon guards your tender silence,
and the stars — they never disclose.

I know you rest in that sacred stillness,
among eternal lights, unseen yet near.
The heavens keep your secret softly,
as if protecting what I hold dear.

Yet I keep walking, heart unwearied,
through dreams, through time, through endless blue —
for when I come home beyond the sky,
the first I'll seek,
will always be you.

16. Thorns and Light

I hold a thorn that blooms,
Its petals cut,
yet scent consumes.
It builds my sky,
then steals my sun,
It is my loss and yet my one.
It breaks me gently,
mends me deep,
It wakes my heart,
then rocks to sleep.
The sweetest ache,
the cruel delight,
My darkest day,
my guiding light.
What am I to do but bleed and bloom-
For joy and sorrow share one room.

17. Embracing the Wound

Do you ever stabbed by a dagger in heart?
The wound which caused can open the light in you!
Where flowers are bloomed wildly later day by day
It may stinks sometimes but embrace you warmly often!
The wounds that you won't regret but cherish every day!

18. October Hurts

There was days in October I was totally felt the magic of
life,
With October rains it made me complete.
Now in this October I'm drenched in this rain
but something deep inside is empty.
I don't know how to fill that void yet—
But I'm trying to fill it with Dandelions,
Which could bloom and fly with the wind,
light as the feather to the sky!
I will always remember the October
which came with a forever,
the magic of my life.

19. Echoes of Us

I wonder — does he still remember me?
The way laughter curled between our words,
the silly things that made the nights feel young,
the hush that only love could speak.

What if it all fades,
like dew leaving no trace on the morning leaf?
What if heaven is light — but memoryless?
Would love still bloom, unnamed, unremembered?

Then why are we born —
to ache, to love, to lose,
if the soul one day drifts empty,
with no whisper of who once held it close?

I pray the heart remembers
what the mind cannot —
that somewhere, beyond forgetting,
his soul still turns toward mine
as if it never learned to let go.

20. Hymn of Earth and Stars

Here rain hums on leaves,
Whispers weave the breeze,
Clouds drift like silver dreams
Beyond the silent seas.
Above, the light breaks slow.
Snow whispers as it glows,
And in the hush of heaven's breath,
Love begins to flow.

Between the worlds they meet,
Raindrops and snowflakes sweet,
A hymn of earth and stars entwined -
Two hearts in endless beat.

21. For the One I Set Free

If you wander again through time,
if your soul forgets me for a while —
may you still find love.
Real love.

The kind that meets you softly,
without questions or conditions.
The kind that holds you when you're tired,
and stays when you're silent.

I won't stand in the way of your joy.
I won't keep you tethered to a memory.
I loved you freely, and I let you go freely —
because my love was never a cage.

And maybe, just maybe,
if you ever feel the wind pause on your cheek,
or a certain silence in the trees —
you'll remember...
someone once loved you like that.

And wished only goodness for you.

Always.